Ruth Thomson

Have You Started Yet?

To Erica,

Enjoy your

womanhood!

Mom,

With love always!

Ruth Thomson

Have You Started Yet?

Illustrated by
Jane Eccles

PAN BOOKS

First published 1980 by Pan Books Ltd.
First revised edition published 1987
This second revised edition published 1995
by Macmillan Children's Books
a division of Macmillan Publishers Ltd
20 New Wharf Road, London N1 9RR
Basingstoke and Oxford
www.panmacmillan.com

Associated companies throughout the world

ISBN 0 330 33722 X

Copyright © Ruth Thomson 1980, 1987, 1995
Illustrations © Jane Eccles 1995

The right of Ruth Thomson & Jane Eccles to be identified as the
author and illustrator of this work has been asserted by them in accordance
with the Copyright, Designs and Patents Act 1988.

14

A CIP catalogue record for this book is available from
the British Library.

Typeset in Gill Sans and Arial
Printed and bound in Great Britain by
Mackays of Chatham plc, Kent

Contents

For my mother

Acknowledgements

The author would like to thank the three hundred or so girls, boys and women whose detailed answers to questionnaires and interviews form the backbone of this book. She would also like to thank the following individuals and organizations for their help, advice, constructive criticism and encouragement: Cynthia Walton, Hazel Slavin, Lynda Measor, Mike Shields, BSc, FRCS, MRCOG, Pam Chrismas, The Kids Book Group (Catherine Brighton, Nicci Crowther, Anita Harper, Ann Heyno, Christine Roche), Bhupinder Sandhu MBBS, MRCP, Gill Haymer, Ruth Parrish, Judy Bastyra, Barry Scherer, Dr Ellen Goudsmit, Pippa Cleator, Gail Chester, Jane Jenks, Elinor Williams, Roy Pennington, Miss J.M. Baugh, Catherine McManus, Roger Lawrence, Nicola Ruck, Robinsons of Chesterfield, Mary Abbott of Kotex Products Advisory Service, Tampax, Grapevine, Janice Saunders, Debbie Miller, Joyce Rosser (Deputy Director of the FPA Education Unit), Dilys Went (Lecturer in Human Biology, University of Warwick), Diane Jameson of Smith and Nephew, Coralie Tiffin, Joan Walsh (Health Policy and Research Officer, FPA), Anna and Judith Shipman, Subashini Puvanendrampillai, Alex Hegazy, Ivana Mackinnon, John Coleman (Director of the Trust for the Study of Adolescence), Joanna Coleman, Alys Fowler.

Introduction
What's in this Book?

This book is about the changes that girls experience some time between the ages of nine and seventeen. It is particularly about periods, something that every woman in the world has for thirty or more years of her life. It will tell you how and why periods happen, what they are like and what to do about them. It gives practical suggestions for dealing with possible difficulties and answers all sorts of questions people often ask.

Before I wrote this, I sent out hundreds of questionnaires, went to lots of schools and interviewed many women, girls and boys to discover what their experiences had been like and to find out what they wanted to know about most. I have included a lot of their quotes throughout the book, so that you can see how enormously experiences and attitudes can differ.

Although this book has been written mainly for girls, it is important that boys should read it too. Girls often feel that periods are a secret they must keep from boys, but the more boys know, the better they will understand girls' feelings and the less embarrassed and awkward they may feel themselves.

Don't feel you have to read the book all at once, straightaway. It's been written for you to use as a reference book, to find out things as and when you need them. Share it with your friends and be bold enough to pass it on to a boy!

I WAS ABOUT ELEVEN. I NOTICED BLOODSPOTS ON MY NIGHTCLOTHES JUST AS I WAS GOING TO BED. I WENT DOWNSTAIRS TO TELL MY MUM I HAD STARTED MY PERIODS.

Chapter 1
Talking About Periods

At some time, usually between the ages of nine and seventeen, girls start having periods. The scientific word for them is **menstruation** (pronounced men-stroo-ay-shun), but people often a use slang word instead — such as time of the month, having the curse, coming on, having the blues, jam butties or the blob.

A girl's first period is a sign that her body is getting ready to be able to have a baby. The thing that tells her that her periods have started is blood appearing from an opening between her legs, called the vagina (to find out what this is, turn to page 25).

Usually blood is a sign that there's something wrong with your body, like a cut or a graze. But when you have a period, there's *nothing* wrong with your body and you haven't hurt yourself. In fact, quite the reverse. Your first period shows you that your body is developing and working in a new way, exactly as it's programmed to do.

Starting your periods doesn't change you overnight, nor does it mean you have to behave any differently from before. It's just one of all the changes that will happen to you as you grow up.

In the time of your great-grandmother, periods were considered very hush-hush and secretive, but these days, people are usually much more open about them. The more you know about periods, the better prepared you'll be when they happen to you. Although this book should give you most of the information you need to know, it's a good idea, if you can, to share your ideas and feelings with someone you're close to, such as your mum, an older sister or cousin, your dad or your gran, just as these girls did.

A girl at school told me she bled regularly and had to wear something to cope with it. She said all girls had it eventually. I couldn't believe it. I thought she had some terrible disease and had been told this story to console her. I told my mum what she had said and asked if it was true. She said it was and told me all about periods.

My sister was really nice to me when I started my periods. We didn't used to get on generally – she was eight years older than me. She gave me a sanitary towel and showed me how to put it on. That was nice. It felt like I was being cared for.

I NEVER REALLY THOUGHT ABOUT THE CHANGES TO MY BODY. THEY HAPPENED AND I ACCEPTED THEM.

Chapter 2

What's Happening to My Body?

U p to about the age of eight or nine, girls and boys look quite alike. They have similar shaped bodies, with no real waist or hips, and slim shoulders. They both have flat chests with small nipples and their voices sound similar. They have the same organs for breathing, moving and digesting food. As they grow, all their organs grow too, but they don't change in any way.

15

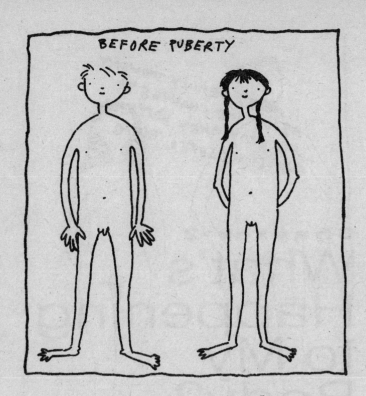

BEFORE PUBERTY

At some time after the age of nine, often at eleven or twelve, boys' and girls' bodies start changing. This time of change is called puberty. The changes mean their bodies are getting ready so that they'll be able to have children when they're older. It doesn't mean everyone will automatically or necessarily have children. That choice will be up to them, when they're ready to make it.

At puberty, a tiny gland at the base of the brain, called the pituitary, sends chemicals, called hormones, into the bloodstream. These reach the sex glands and start them working. In girls, these glands are called ovaries and in boys, the testicles. These glands, in turn, start to produce hormones of their own, which

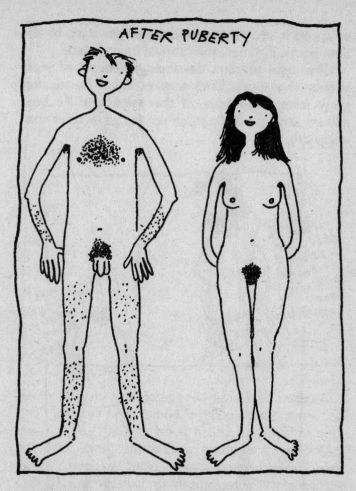

AFTER PUBERTY

trigger off all the sexual changes to the rest of the body. As a result, men and women end up looking different.

The changes don't happen to everyone at the same time. You might develop sooner or later than your friends, sisters or brothers. Each person has his or her own in-built body timetable, and grows and changes at their own pace. There's nothing you can do to speed it up. Whenever the changes start, by the time you're eighteen, they should be complete.

Girls tend to start developing a couple of years sooner than boys. Until they're fifteen or so, they grow faster than boys of the same age. As boys mature, they gradually catch up and grow taller than many girls.

Before puberty you grow so slowly, year by year, that you've probably scarcely even been aware of growing. At puberty, you'll notice a sudden surge and, in a way, you have to get to know your body all over again. As you become aware of your own body, you'll probably also become more aware of other people's.

You may worry that some bit of you isn't quite how you'd like it to be, but just remember that almost everyone else is worrying too!

I FELT 'ROUND' AND WANTED TO BE 'STRAIGHT'.

I WAS TALL, THIN AND FLAT-CHESTED. I LONGED TO GROW SOME CURVES.

I HATED MY BREASTS FOR BEING SO SMALL.

I WAS BOTHERED THAT MY BREASTS WERE LARGER THAN THE OTHER GIRLS' IN MY CLASS.

What particular changes happen to boys?

Boys grow taller and stronger and their feet grow bigger. Their shoulders broaden, their chest widens and muscles start to develop. The penis and testicles (the male sex organs) start to grow bigger and pubic hair starts sprouting. The testicles start producing sperm (the male seeds). Often, the skin around the testicles reddens and coarsens.

As boys continue to grow, their vocal chords grow. This eventually makes their voices deeper, although they may squeak from time to time at first. Hair starts growing under their arms, on their faces and perhaps on their chest as well. The hair on their arms and legs grows thicker and darker and their pubic hair becomes thick and curly. Their skin and sweat glands start working.

What particular changes happen to girls?

Girls grow taller and heavier as well. Their faces become fuller; their hips become wider and rounder, their breasts start to develop and pubic hair starts to appear. Their sex organs start to change.

As they develop more, girls start having periods, their breasts fill out, underarm hair starts appearing, their sweat glands become active and their skin gets oilier.

All about breasts

Growing breasts is one of the first changes you're likely to notice. The nipples become larger, darker and stand out. They may become very sensitive to touch. Actual breasts develop gradually. Some girls notice a tingling feeling or occasional soreness. This is quite normal and has to do with their growing.

Breasts, like other parts of the body, come in all shapes and sizes. There's no such thing as 'perfect' breasts, even if magazines and advertisements try to persuade you otherwise. If your mother and female relatives (on either your mother's or father's side) have small or large breasts, the chances are that your breasts will end up a similar size to theirs.

If you have small breasts and have had periods for some years, your breasts are unlikely to grow much bigger. If you've only just started your periods, or not started yet, and your breasts are growing, you can expect them to grow some more.

Breasts don't always grow evenly. Sometimes one grows faster than the other. Don't worry about it — they will even out in time. It's unlikely, in any case, that they will ever match up exactly. Your hands and the sides of your face don't match up exactly either, but who worries about those?

Girls are often concerned about growing breasts – what's a pleasure for one is agony for another . . .

I felt very proud. I measured their growth regularly and really looked forward to wearing a bra.

I didn't really like my breasts growing. I knew I'd have to wear a bra and I felt embarrassed.

I HAD BREASTS AT TEN AND WAS AMAZED HOW JEALOUS SOME GIRLS WERE IF THEY DIDN'T HAVE BREASTS AS LARGE AS THE NEXT GIRL. WE ALL COMPARED SHAPES AND SIZES.

I WAS COMPLETELY
FLAT-CHESTED UNTIL I WAS
15. I THOUGHT I'D NEVER
GROW BREASTS AT ALL.

Girls who develop early sometimes feel self-conscious, while girls who develop later feel left out.
But whatever size your breasts end up, there's not much point in worrying about how you match up with anyone else. You're stuck with them, so you should try and accept them, however hard that might seem to begin with.

It was worrying at first to have a small bust compared with others. But now I've grown to realize that a small bust runs in my family.

Your sex organs

As well as your changing size and shape, some parts of you develop in new ways. For instance, your external sex organs, known as the vulva, become larger and more sensitive. If you've never had a close look at your vulva before, it's worth spending a quiet moment getting to know what it's like and then seeing how it changes. The more you get to know and value your body, the better you'll feel about it. You'll also find it useful if you want to try using tampons during your periods (see page 46).

Make sure you're not in a rush and have a bit of privacy and clean hands. You'll need a mirror and a good light. Sit on the floor, or a bed, with your legs apart and your knees bent. Hold the mirror up between your legs and prop this book where you can see it easily. See if you can identify everything from the picture overleaf. Remember though, girls' vulvas differ as much as every other part of their bodies, so your vulva might not look exactly like this one. Your lips might be bigger or smaller or you may not have a hymen.

➤ **The mons** is a fatty pad which protects the pubic bone inside. It becomes covered with pubic hair.

➤ **The outer lips** are folds of fatty tissue, which protect the inner area and keep it moist and healthy. They become covered with pubic hair on the outside. During puberty, they gradually become larger, darker, fleshier and sensitive to touch.

➤ **The inner lips** are the folds of tissue you will see if you gently part the outer lips. They are hairless, moist and may be pink or brown. Usually they lie

23

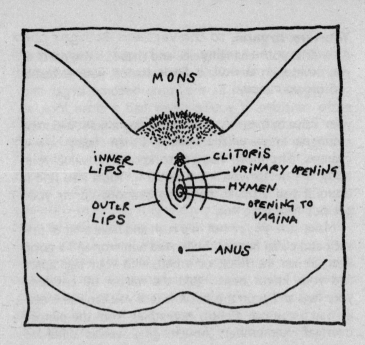

together and protect the opening during puberty. You may have inner lips which stick out beyond the outer ones, one lip longer than the other or very small ones.

All of these are quite normal. At the top of the lips, the folds are joined together and cover the clitoris.

➤ **The clitoris** is the most sensitive part of your vulva. You'll only be able to see its tip, a bump about the size of a pea. The rest is hidden under the inner lips. If you can't find the clitoris, gently press around where you think it should be. When you notice a pleasant sensation, you've probably found it.

➤ **The urinary opening** (also known as the urethra) is a tiny hole just below the clitoris, where your pee comes out.

➤ **The opening to the vagina** is the bigger opening below the urethra. It looks quite small, but can stretch a great deal. It leads to the uterus (womb) inside your body.

➤ **The hymen** is a thin stretchy fold of skin which may partly cover the opening to the vagina. Usually there are one or more openings in it through which blood can flow during a period. In the past, people thought they could tell a girl was a virgin if her hymen was unbroken. In fact, many girls are born without a hymen at all. These days, a girl's hymen is often stretched or broken quite naturally by exercise, such as jumping or riding a bike. Virginity has nothing to do with whether you've got a hymen or not. You stop being a virgin only when you have sexual intercourse.

➤ **The anus** is the opening through which solid waste comes out of your body. It is not part of your sex organs.

Pubic and body hair

When your pubic hair first starts growing, it is soft and colourless. Eventually it darkens and coarsens. It is usually darker than the hair on your head, or may be a different colour altogether. Some girls have quite thick pubic hair, others have only a scanty amount.

Hair will also start growing under your arms and on your arms and legs as well. It is not uncommon for girls to find hair growing around their nipples and across their tummies as well.

I USED TO THINK THAT PERIODS WERE JUST SOMETHING EXTERNAL THAT HAPPENED. NOW I REALIZE THAT THEY'RE PART OF ALL THE OTHER CHANGES THAT ARE TAKING PLACE.

Chapter 3

What's Happening Inside My Body?

All about your reproductive organs

As well as all the changes you can see happening, other important changes — ones you can't see — are happening *inside* your body at the same time. The reproductive organs which you were born with start to grow and develop. Each one is designed to play a part in produdng a new life — whether or not they ever do so.

THE REPRODUCTIVE ORGANS ARE WELL PROTECTED INSIDE YOUR BODY. TO FIND OUT PRECISELY WHERE THEY ARE, PUT YOUR FOREFINGERS ON THE BONE JUST ABOVE WHERE YOUR LEGS MEET.

NOW PUT YOUR THUMBS ON THE FRONT OF YOUR HIP BONES. YOUR REPRODUCTIVE ORGANS ARE ENCLOSED INSIDE THIS BONY AREA. THEY ARE OF A SIMILAR SIZE FOR EVERYONE REGARDLESS OF BODY SIZE.

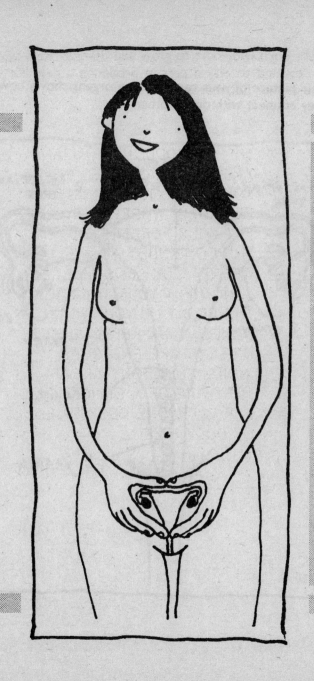

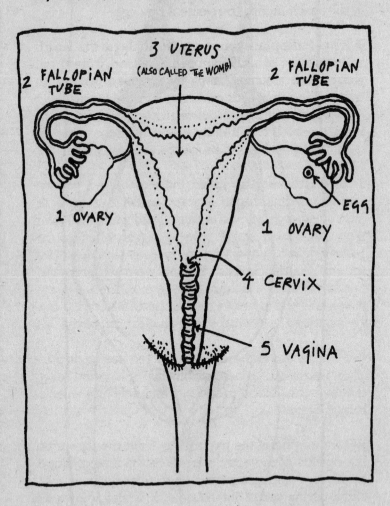

This picture of your reproductive organs shows how they connect with one another.

1 The ovaries are both about the size and shape of an almond. They are storehouses for thousands of minute egg-cells (called ova), which girls are born with. Once a girl reaches puberty, the ovaries take it in turn each month to release a ripe egg.

2 The Fallopian tubes are both about the length and thickness of a ballpoint pen. One end, fringed and shaped like a funnel, is partly wrapped around an ovary. The other ends open out into the uterus.

When an egg comes out of an ovary, the fringes of the tube catch it and draw it into the tube. The egg then travels through the tube towards the uterus.

3 The uterus (also called the womb) is a hollow, stretchy organ, shaped like an upside-down pear. It has strong walls of muscle and is lined with glands and blood vessels. It starts growing bigger when you're about ten and by the time you are eighteen, it will be the size of a clenched fist. When a woman is pregnant, this is where the unborn baby grows. During pregnancy, the uterus grows to the size of a netball — but goes back to its normal size again after the birth.

4 The cervix is the entrance to the uterus. It usually stays closed. It opens slightly during a period to let the menstrual blood trickle out, and only fully when a baby is born.

5 The vagina is the passageway from the uterus to the outside of the body. It is where the flow of blood comes out during a period. It is where a penis will enter during sexual intercourse. It is also known as the birth canal. Its walls of soft, folded skin stretch very easily to allow a baby to be born.

The life of an egg-cell

Once you start having periods, this is what happens inside your body every month.

The Menstrual Cycle

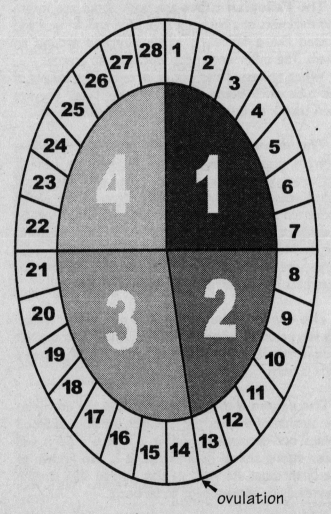

ovulation

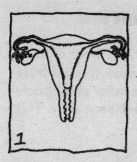

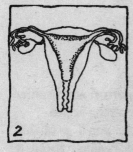

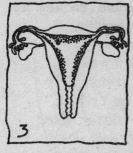

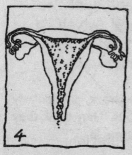

1 At about the time your period stops, a tiny egg-cell starts to ripen in one of the ovaries. The following month, an egg-cell will ripen in the other ovary.

2 The ovary sends a hormone signal to the uterus. The lining of the uterus begins to thicken. About fourteen days after your last period, the ripe egg bursts out of the ovary. This is called ovulation.

3 The egg travels down a Fallopian tube towards the uterus. By now the lining of the uterus has become thick and spongy to make a soft bed for the egg if it becomes fertilized. But the *only* way an egg can become fertilized is if it joins with a sperm, and this can only happen if you have sex with a male just after ovulation.

4 If the egg is *not* fertilized, your body knows that it doesn't need the spongy lining, which breaks down. The blood vessels contract, causing bleeding. The lining and the remains of the egg flow out of the uterus and through your vagina. This is your period.

What will my first period feel like?

There's no one answer to this question. It varies from girl to girl. There is one sign that many girls notice, which often means their periods will soon start. This is how one girl describes it:

> Six months before I started, I sometimes got a slight white discharge which stained my knickers — we called it 'the whites'.

This is a vaginal discharge and is a normal and healthy sign that the sex hormones are becoming active.

Like any other first experience, you'll probably always remember your first period. Feelings about it differ widely. Some girls feel excited, because it's something they've been looking forward to.

> I had my first period when I was eleven. I was watching TV in my nightie. When I got up to go to bed, there was blood on it. My sister, aged ten, said, 'You lucky thing, you've started your periods.' I went upstairs and put on a sanitary towel (which I'd practised doing before). I told everyone who would listen. I felt very proud.

For other girls, it can be a terrible shock, particularly if no one has told them about periods. They think they must have hurt themselves or become ill.

I WOKE UP ONE MORNING TO FIND BLOOD ON THE SHEETS. IT GAVE ME A TERRIBLE FRIGHT, AS I DIDN'T KNOW WHERE IT CAME FROM. I THOUGHT I WAS BLEEDING TO DEATH INSIDE. I DIDN'T KNOW IT WAS A PERIOD. NO ONE HAD TOLD ME ABOUT THEM.

Sometimes, even if a girl knows about periods, her first one comes as a surprise, without any warning.

I went to the toilet and there it was – blood on my knickers.

I woke up one morning and there was blood on my bed.

Quite a few girls do have a warning that something is happening – even if they don't know what it is.

One night I had strange cramps and couldn't sleep. When I got up the next morning, I went to the loo and found blood.

I had an ache low down in my tummy and felt tired and then my period started.

I felt uncomfortable and as if I wanted to pee all the time. I didn't feel ill, but I didn't feel well. Then I discovered my periods had started.

No one's first period is exactly the same. When your first period happens, it might be long or short, painful or painless and the flow may be red, rusty or brown. See how these girls' experiences differed.

It was very, very dark brown and very smooth and very thick.

It wasn't red like real blood. It only lasted a day or two.

I bled for two whole weeks. I couldn't believe it.

I was surprised that it didn't hurt and by the way the blood came out bit by bit and didn't pour out as I had expected.

I had bad stomach aches in gym, but I didn't notice any blood until I got home. It was a kind of rusty colour.

What do I need to do when I start?

The most important thing to remember is that periods happen to every single girl and woman and that there's no need to panic or to feel shy about asking for help. Most women will be very sympathetic and do their best to help you. Periods can start at any time and not necessarily when you're best prepared for them. You're most likely to notice you've started when you're in the loo and see bloodstains on your pants. If you're at home, your mum or sister or gran can show you what to do. If you're at school, ask the school nurse, a teacher or a friend for help.

> I went to the loo and there was some blood. I yelled for my mum and she came and fixed me up with a pad.

> I started in the swimming pool at school. I had a stomach ache and could see blood coming out of me. I got out and told the man teacher I was going to the toilet. I saw a woman teacher and told her I'd started. She gave me a pad.

If you're somewhere where you feel it's impossible to ask for help, you can always make do (see page 60). But if you can talk to someone, you'll avoid having experiences like these.

> I was staying with a friend. In the morning, I found blood when I went to

the loo. I knew what it was, but I didn't know what to do. I had no sanitary towels or anything and I was too shy to ask or tell anyone. I stuffed toilet paper in my pants and hoped that all my layers of clothes would keep the blood hidden. It was a miserable day. I couldn't relax or think of anything else.

I got a towel out of a machine in the school toilets. It was folded in a square. I didn't know how to put it on. So I put it in my pants just as it was — in a small square. When I got home, Mum showed me what to do.

What's a normal period?

There's no such thing! The only thing that's certain is that periods start and stop by themselves. Some may last two days, some may last eight days. Some people have periods every twenty-one days and some people have them every thirty-five days. Most people have them somewhere in between. Sometimes periods are heavy, sometimes they're light. Sometimes the flow may be heaviest for the first two days and then taper off and sometimes it might be exactly the opposite. The colour of the flow may change too. It often starts rusty red, becomes bright red when the flow is fastest and then turns brownish by the end.

How often will I have periods?

For the first two years after your periods start, there will probably be no regular pattern to them. It's quite OK to have a period once every three, four, five or even every six weeks, or to have a period one month and not the next.

After a couple of years, you should begin to notice a more regular pattern to your periods, as your hormones settle down. If you're worried that you don't have a regular pattern, see page 94 for more information about irregular and interrupted periods. You might also like to keep a record of your cycle on the calendar on pages 64–65.

I USE PADS BECAUSE IT'S EASY TO KNOW WHEN TO CHANGE THEM...

I USE TAMPONS BECAUSE THEY'RE HIDDEN AWAY AND NO ONE CAN TELL WHEN I'VE GOT MY PERIOD...

Chapter 4
Towels and Tampons

Once you start having periods, you'll need to wear something to catch the flow of blood. The flow is usually a slow trickle with an occasional spurt. You can't control it. Unlike peeing, a period happens automatically and continues both day and night. To avoid staining your clothes, you can use either sanitary towels (also known as pads) or tampons.

Towels

Sanitary towels are soft, absorbent pads, which you put inside your pants. They have a leak-proof plastic backing with a sticky strip so you can press them firmly in place on your pants.

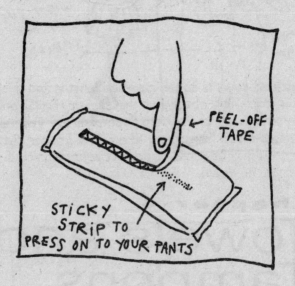

PEEL-OFF TAPE

STICKY STRIP TO PRESS ON TO YOUR PANTS

Towels come in different sizes and shapes. You might like to try out several kinds to see which ones you like using the best. Some manufacturers will send free samples if you write to them, so you can try out several brands and see which suit you best. Their addresses are on pages 101–102.

Pant liners are the thinnest. You might like to use these on the day you expect your period to start or at the end of your period when the flow is very light.

PANT LINER

Standard towels come in several lengths and thicknesses. You will probably find that slim or regular ones give you enough protection. Superpads are generally for women who have a very heavy flow. Longer nighttime ones may be useful to protect your night-clothes when you lie down.

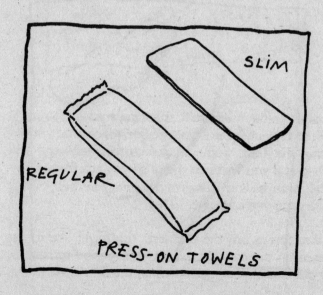

SLIM

REGULAR

PRESS-ON TOWELS

Shaped towels are wider at the front than at the back and have extra padding in the middle. The ends are thin and rounded to make the towels less bulky.

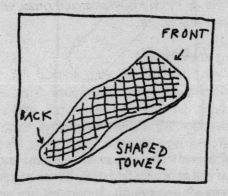

FRONT

BACK

SHAPED TOWEL

Winged towels have sticky 'wings' which fold under the pants to stop the towel moving.

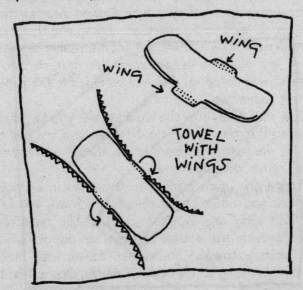

WING

WING

TOWEL WITH WINGS

Buying towels

You can buy towels in chemists, supermarkets and many corner shops. They come either in packets of loose towels or individually wrapped ones, which are ideal for carrying about.

Changing your towel

For the first few days of your period, it's best to change your towel every few hours. This will help prevent stains, unpleasant smells, sore thighs or any risk of infection. It's easiest to change them in the lavatory. Remember to wash your hands before and afterwards.

Getting rid of used towels

Look at the instructions on the packet to find out what you have to do with the kind of towels you use. The ones that say 'completely disposable' are the most convenient – they can be flushed away as they are. Some need to be pulled apart first, and the parts flushed separately. Others are not disposable in water at all and *must* be thrown away. It's best to throw towels away rolled up and well wrapped in loo paper or in a paper bag.

Ask your mum how she would prefer you to get rid of towels at home. If in doubt when you are out or staying the night away from home, throw used towels away, rather than flush them.

There are often notices in lavatories in schools, cinemas and other public places, which ask you not to flush away any type of towel. Public lavatories often provide paper bags and bins or disposal units for sanitary towels. Sometimes towels can block up the plumbing, so it's best to use the disposal facilities provided.

Tampons

A tampon is a tight roll of cotton fibres with a cord attached to one end. You push it into your vagina and leave it there to soak up the period flow *inside* your body. It expands gently, both in length and width, inside the vagina, but you shouldn't be able to feel that it's there at all.

There are two kinds of tampons – those with cardboard applicators, which help you guide the tampon into place, and those without applicators, which you push in place with your fingers.

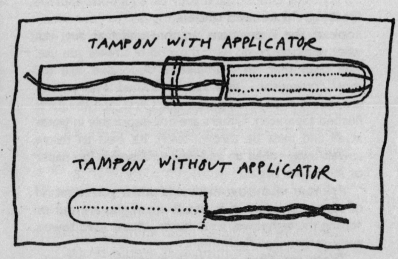

TAMPON WITH APPLICATOR

TAMPON WITHOUT APPLICATOR

Tampons come in several sizes – small, extra-thin mini-tampons, designed specifically for younger girls; regular and super. It's important to use the lowest absorbency tampon for your flow when you start. Begin with mini tampons. If they become fully absorbed in *less* than four hours, you need to use regular or super ones instead. But, if you take out a regular or super tampon after a few hours and there is a lot of white fibre showing, use mini-ones instead.

When to use tampons
There's no set age for starting to use tampons. It's up to you to decide when you're ready. Some girls may find it difficult to insert a tampon at first and may prefer to use towels until they've got used to having regular periods.

Some parents have strong feelings about girls using tampons and this may be a touchy subject. If you want to try using tampons and your parents don't approve, or if you think they might object, talk to your friends instead. See if they use tampons and find out what they think of them.

I bought a packet of tampons to try. I couldn't get the hang of them. I asked my mum for advice. She said I was too young to use them. A few months later, I went to stay with a friend, who suggested that we went swimming. I said I had my period and couldn't. My friend used mini-tampons. She asked her mum if it would be OK if I used them. She said, 'Yes, by all means, they're perfectly harmless.' This surprised me after my mum's reaction. Anyway, I tried them and I've used them ever since.

Discovering your vagina

If you have a problem putting in your first tampon, it's probably because you don't know your body well enough.

> The main problem was that I didn't really know where my vagina was, so I didn't know where the tampon went.

> I had an idea that my vagina was very narrow and that anything going in or coming out would hurt — happily I discovered that quite the opposite is the case.

If you want to use tampons, it's a good idea to get a feel of what your vagina is like first. Do this when you are relaxed and have a quiet moment on your own, perhaps after a warm bath. **Wash your hands**, before parting the lips of your vulva and putting a finger or two inside your vagina. Feel which direction the vagina goes in. Can you feel that it goes at an angle, more towards your back than straight up? This is the angle to aim at when you put in a tampon. Feel the muscles of the vagina walls. These will hold the tampon securely in place.

Putting in a tampon

When you decide you're ready to try putting in a tampon, make sure you're relaxed and have plenty of time and privacy. If you're tense and in a hurry, your muscles will tighten up! The best time to try is actually *during* a period, not between periods. You may find it easiest of all during the first two days of a period when the flow is usually heaviest. It's far easier to slide a tampon into a moist vagina than into a dry one. If you find you can't get the tampon in, don't worry. Wait a month or so and then try again until you succeed.

I was really scared and didn't push them high enough at first. Now they're OK.

I think I pushed the tampons in too gently at first. I became frustrated when they didn't magically slot into place. It took quite a while before I got the hang of it.
It took me six months before my muscles stopped tensing around them. Now I get on with them fine.

Every packet of tampons contains a leaflet which explains exactly how to put them in. Read it carefully before you try. The instructions may seem complicated at first. Once you get used to putting in a tampon, you will be able to do it in a matter of seconds.
You may like to read the simplified instructions on the following pages so you can see what's involved.

How to use a tampon without an applicator

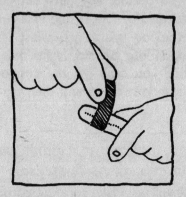

1 Wash your hands. Unwrap the colour tear-strip and the cellopane cover. Gently pull the cord to make sure it is firmly in place. Check that the ends are tied together. If you drop the tampon on the floor by mistake, don't use it!

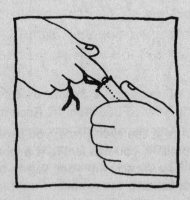

2 Flare out the cord end of the tampon, making a little dimple to put your first finger in.

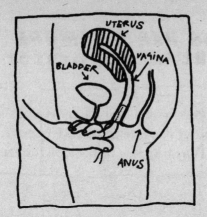

3 Rest one foot on the toilet seat, bath or a chair. Gently push the tampon with your finger as far into the vagina as it will go. Make sure the cord is hanging outside your body.

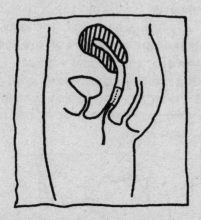

4 If the tampon is in the right place, you shouldn't be able to feel it at all. (If you can feel it, it probably isn't in far enough.) The muscles in your vagina hold it in place, so it can't fall out.

To remove it, gently pull on the cord at the same angle as when you put it in. The tampon will slide out and you can flush it away.

How to use a tampon with an applicator

Some tampons have a pair of card tubes (which fit together rather like a telescope). These are called an applicator. They help you to position the tampon.

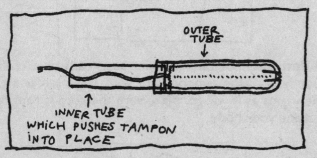

OUTER TUBE

INNER TUBE WHICH PUSHES TAMPON INTO PLACE

1 Unwrap a tampon. Make sure the cord is showing outside the smaller tube. Stand with one foot on the toilet seat or a chair or crouch down with your knees apart. Hold the larger tube (which contains the tampon) at the grooves. With your other hand spread the lips of your vulva apart.

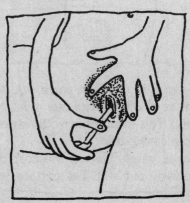

2 Push the outer tube gently into your vagina. Point it towards the small of your back. Don't force it in further than it will go easily. Push it until most of the outer tube is in your vagina.

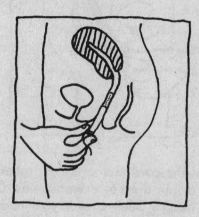

3 Keep holding the outer tube. Put your forefinger over the end of the inner tube to hold the cord in place. Push the inner tube completely into the outer tube, so the ends are level. This pushes the tampon out of the tube and into the vagina.

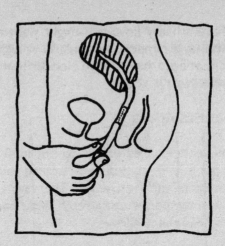

4 Let go of the cord. Remove both tubes and flush them away or put them in a disposal unit. Check that the cord is hanging freely outside your body.

When you need to change the tampon, gently pull the cord to remove it at the same angle as when you put it in. You can flush it away.

Changing tampons

You need to change a tampon every few hours or so, especially for the first few days of your period, when the flow is usually the heaviest. You can tell when a tampon needs changing, because you will notice a kind of bubbling feeling at the base of your vagina or you will see that the cord is bloodstained. Always use a fresh tampon before you go to bed and when you get up. Never leave one in for more than eight hours.

Make absolutely sure that you've removed a used tampon, before you put in a new one, and don't forget to take out the last tampon of a period. If you notice a smell, even though you've washed thoroughly, check to see whether you've left in a tampon.

If you have a heavy flow, you might want to use a towel as well as a tampon, particularly at night. If the tampon cannot absorb any more blood, the towel will catch any dribbles.

Facts about tampons

➤ Tampons shouldn't be painful to put in. If it hurts when you put one in, it's probably because you haven't aimed it at quite the right angle. The vagina is very stretchy – remember, it can stretch wide enough to let a baby's head come through.

➤ Tampons can't get 'lost' inside you. The opening to the uterus is so tiny, that it is impossible for a tampon to go through it. A tampon will always stay in the vagina. There is *nowhere* else for it to go (see the picture on page 30)

➤ Once a tampon is in place, you shouldn't be able to feel it at all. If you can, you haven't pushed it in far enough. Either try pushing it in further with your finger or pull it out and try again with a new one.

➤ If, by mistake, you push the cord up into your vagina, you can still pull out the tampon. Squat down and put your first two fingers (well washed) into your vagina. If you can't reach the tampon, try straining hard, as if you were going to the toilet. Then you should be able to grasp it. If you still can't reach it, try again in the bath or ask someone to help you. Doctors are quite used to taking out tampons.

➤ A very rare disease, called Toxic Shock Syndrome, has been linked with using tampons. It starts like the flu – the symptoms are a sudden high temperature, of 102°F (39°C) or more, sickness and diarrhoea, a sore throat, dizziness and a rash that looks like sunburn. If you get any of these symptoms while you're using a tampon, take it out straightaway and call the doctor.

Which to use?

Both towels and tampons have their advantages and disadvantages. You'll need to try both to discover which you find easier and more comfortable to use. Here's what several girls say about them.

Advantages

Towels

AT NIGHT I WEAR A TOWEL. IT'S MORE COMFORTABLE AND GIVES BETTER PROTECTION. IN THE DAY I WEAR TAMPONS.

They're discreet, secure and I feel confident wearing them.

They are comfortable and most of them are flushable. I don't think I'd like to try tampons yet. They frighten me a little, but I don't know why.

They are easy to dispose of and you know when to change them.

Tampons

TAMPONS ARE CLEAN AND EASY AND DON'T TAKE UP TOO MUCH SPACE IN A BAG. THEY'RE EASY TO PACK WHEN I GO AWAY SOMEWHERE.

Using tampons makes a period easier. They're invisible. There's no worrying about smells or disposal. They make me feel more comfortable and relaxed.

I like tampons because they get rid of that messy feeling, but I think they're expensive.

Disadvantages

Towels

THEY'RE ALWAYS THERE AND YOU CAN'T FORGET THEM. YOU CAN'T GO SWIMMING OR ANYTHING LIKE THAT.

They're bulky and horrid. They make me shudder.

I always worry about the smell if I can't change them often enough.

They sometimes slip out of place and rub the top of my thighs.

Tampons

I can't always control my bladder with a tampon in and I find it hard to put them in when my flow is light.

For the first two days a tampon isn't enough for the night-time. I use a towel as well, held in place with knickers.

I FIND IT DIFFICULT TO TELL WHEN TO CHANGE THEM – SOMETIMES I FEEL THEM LEAKING AND THEN IT'S TOO LATE.

Just occasionally, I find I get the angle wrong when I'm putting one in. It kind of bends over and becomes uncomfortable – in which case I replace it with another.

You might find it interesting to compare the advertisements for different kinds of towels and tampons to see which advantages each one claims. Sometimes they play on people's fears of things showing, bad smells or leaking. If you change whatever you use fairly often, especially during the first two days of a period, you shouldn't need to worry about any of those things.

Be prepared

Make a note in your diary or calendar of the first day of your period, so you know roughly when the next one will happen. Around that time, it's a good idea to carry a towel or a tampon with you, when you're out or at school. You may even prefer to wear a pant liner, in case your period starts when you're nowhere near a toilet.

If your periods are very irregular, or if it would help you feel more prepared, you could always keep a spare towel or tampon in your school bag or in your locker.

A spare pair of pants is useful as well. Even if you don't need the towel or tampon, you may find it comes in handy for one of your friends.

Sometimes your period may start when you least expect it. If you have nothing with you, you can always use tissues, folded sheets of toilet paper, or a clean hanky. Use them like a sanitary towel.

Don't feel embarrassed to ask other girls or women if they have a spare towel or tampon you can use. They all have periods too, so they'll be sympathetic. If you start at school, either the medical room or the office is usually the place to go for supplies. Some schools and public toilets have slot machines where you can buy individual towels or tampons.

...IF YOU DON'T NEED THE PAD OR TAMPON YOU MAY FIND IT COMES IN HANDY FOR ONE OF YOUR FRIENDS.

Chapter 5
You and Your Cycle

Periods are only one part of the menstrual cycle. Since they're the part that seems most noticeable, people often don't bother to think about what's happening to them during the rest of their cycle.

But perhaps you've noticed that on some days you feel great, have bags of energy and your skin and hair look good. Then, on other days, you feel awful – you can't concentrate properly, you snap at your parents and friends, feel depressed with the way you look and cry more easily.

Sometimes, of course, there is a good reason for how you feel. Maybe you've had a celebration or a disappointment, or perhaps you've been complimented or told off. But sometimes you can't see any reason at all for your feelings. There is one! It's all to do with your menstrual cycle.

Work out the length of your cycle
The length of your cycle is the number of days

January						
1	2	3	4	5	6	7
8	9	10	11	12	13	14
15	16	17	18	19	20	21
22	23	24	25	26	27	28
29	30	31				

February						
1	2	3	4	5	6	7
8	9	10	11	12	13	14
15	16	17	18	19	20	21
22	23	24	25	26	27	28
(29)						

March						
1	2	3	4	5	6	7
8	9	10	11	12	13	14
15	16	17	18	19	20	21
22	23	24	25	26	27	28
29	30	31				

April						
1	2	3	4	5	6	7
8	9	10	11	12	13	14
15	16	17	18	19	20	21
22	23	24	25	26	27	28
29	30					

May						
1	2	3	4	5	6	7
8	9	10	11	12	13	14
15	16	17	18	19	20	21
22	23	24	25	26	27	28
29	30	31				

June						
1	2	3	4	5	6	7
8	9	10	11	12	13	14
15	16	17	18	19	20	21
22	23	24	25	26	27	28
29	30					

between the start of one period and the next. It may be as short as twenty-one days, as long as thirty-five days, or anything in-between. All are quite normal. When you first start your periods, your cycle is quite likely to be *very* irregular. Use this calendar to help you work out your own cycle. Circle the day you start a period and cross through each day it lasts.

July

1	2	3	4	5	6	7
8	9	10	11	12	13	14
15	16	17	18	19	20	21
22	23	24	25	26	27	28
29	30	31				

August

1	2	3	4	5	6	7
8	9	10	11	12	13	14
15	16	17	18	19	20	21
22	23	24	25	26	27	28
29	30	31				

September

1	2	3	4	5	6	7
8	9	10	11	12	13	14
15	16	17	18	19	20	21
22	23	24	25	26	27	28
29	30					

October

1	2	3	4	5	6	7
8	9	10	11	12	13	14
15	16	17	18	19	20	21
22	23	24	25	26	27	28
29	30	31				

November

1	2	3	4	5	6	7
8	9	10	11	12	13	14
15	16	17	18	19	20	21
22	23	24	25	26	27	28
29	30					

December

1	2	3	4	5	6	7
8	9	10	11	12	13	14
15	16	17	18	19	20	21
22	23	24	25	26	27	28
29	30	31				

Personal Mood Chart

Keep a chart of your feelings

Find out whether and how your cycle affects you by keeping a chart of your feelings. After three or four months, you should be able to see whether any particular feelings happen again and again at the same intervals. Even if you haven't started your periods yet, you may still be able to see a pattern.

Filling in your chart

➤ Mark each day of your period with a **P**.
➤ Mark days when your flow is heavier with an **H**.
➤ Note the days when you feel particularly good or bad with your own symbols, pictures or words.
➤ Weigh yourself the week before and after a period to see if there is any noticeable difference.

MONTH ONE
1
2
3
4
5
6
7
8
9
10
11
12
13
14
15
16
17
18
19
20
21
22
23
24
25
26
27
28
29
30
31

MONTH TWO		MONTH THREE	
1		1	
2		2	
3		3	
4		4	
5		5	
6		6	
7		7	
8		8	
9		9	
10		10	
11		11	
12		12	
13		13	
14		14	
15		15	
16		16	
17		17	
18		18	
19		19	
20		20	
21		21	
22		22	
23		23	
24		24	
25		25	
26		26	
27		27	
28		28	
29		29	
30		30	
31		31	

Everybody is different
Nobody's cycle is exactly the same. You might find that you have no noticeable pattern at all to yours.

I don't notice any changes in mood due to my periods. I'm very moody anyway and my moods change from hour to hour and day to day without any reason that I can see.

My moods are more affected by whether I have a good or bad day at school and have a good or bad social life than by my periods.

On the other hand, you might feel OK most of the time, except around the time of your period.

Sometimes my nipples hurt the day before a period. I get constipated for the first few days and I get cramps.

OUCH!

I'M A BIT CLUMSY DURING MY PERIOD - I SEEM TO GET A LOT OF CUTS AND SCRATCHES ON MY HANDS...

I feel I can't do much when I have periods and I get annoyed.

You may notice that your moods change noticeably at different times of the month.

I feel very high after a period, then, just when I think I'm going to do great things in the next few weeks, I get low. Now I know what it is, I try to plan for it.

Or you might feel good for most of your cycle except for the week or so before your period is due. Then you might notice changes to your body, such as:

I can't bear to be touched.

MY STOMACH FEELS BLOATED. I GET STOMACH AND BACK ACHE...

My hair gets greasier more quickly and so does my skin.

My breasts swell and my tummy feels tender. I feel heavy and overweight and get spots.

Your moods may change at the same time.

I'm miserable a week before I'm due. I behave a bit quiet.

I feel stupid and slow.

I feel grumpy, uncomfortable and cry easily.

I'm impatient and snap at people for no reason.

Helpful suggestions

The body and mood changes which happen before a period are called PMS, which is short for Pre-Menstrual Syndrome. No one knows for certain why these changes happen, but they're very common. If they bother you, some of the following suggestions may help.

➤ I feel bloated and fat when I've got a period.

If you put on a few pounds when you've got a period, you are probably retaining extra water. Cut down on salty foods, which help retain water, and don't drink caffeinated drinks, such as coffee, tea, or fizzy soft drinks.

➤ I get snappy
and can't seem to help it.

If you get cross, irritable or panicky for no real reason or suddenly feel weak, particularly in the week before a period, notice whether this happens when you haven't eaten for a long time. If so, eat snacks at short intervals throughout the day, as well as your usual meals, to give you extra energy.

If you feel especially tired or lazy, try to get some extra rest and sleep in the fortnight before your period is due. It may also help to eat plenty of fruit and vegetables, wholemeal bread, nuts and seeds. If you have sweet food cravings, eat peanuts or peanut butter and ripe bananas, and drink fresh orange juice, herbal teas and lots of water, rather than binge on biscuits or sweets.

➤ I put off anything
   that can possibly be
   left until after my period.

I SAVE UP NICE THINGS TO DO FOR DAYS WHEN I FEEL DOWN — A GOOD BOOK, KNITTING, MAKING THINGS, LISTENING TO MY FAVOURITE MUSIC . . . .

If you keep a chart of how you feel, you can work out the days when you might feel a bit down. Then you can prepare for them and not arrange too many busy social events. You may also find that once you know *why* you're feeling a certain way, you can cope better with those feelings anyway.

If none of these suggestions help, it's worth going to see your doctor. Take your chart with you. It will help the doctor see how your symptoms relate to your cycle.

Chapter 6
Be Nice to Yourself

As you grow up, the hormones that cause your periods to start also affect other parts of your body, as well as your moods, your appetite and your energy. You'll need to start looking after yourself in ways you never had to bother about when you were younger.

Keep clean

You have sweat glands all over your skin. When you get hot, your body perspires to help cool you down. The perspiration is a mixture of water and salt and doesn't smell. At puberty, new sweat glands develop under the arms, around the nipples, navel and in the inner lips of the vulva. These are scent glands, which give you your individual smell, but if you get too hot and sweaty, the smell becomes rather stale.

TO KEEP YOURSELF
SMELLING FRESH, HAVE
A DAILY WARM SHOWER
OR BATH...

To keep yourself smelling fresh, have a warm shower or bath daily. Remember to wash particularly under your arms and between your legs. Always wash your vulva and bottom from front to back, so you don't infect your vagina with any of the germs from the anus. This also applies to wiping your bottom after going to the loo — always front to back.

After a wash or bath, change into clean pants. Cotton ones are best, because synthetic ones tend to keep in heat and moisture unless they have a cotton gusset.

You may like to start using an underarm deodorant – particularly during a period when your sweat glands are more active.

Keeping clean during a period
You may hear people say you shouldn't wash your hair or have a bath when you've got a period. Rubbish! They're old wives' tales.

It's quite OK to have a bath, so long as it's not too hot. The flow stops while you're sitting in the water. If you use tampons, you can leave one in while you're bathing, but put in a clean one afterwards. If you use sanitary towels, make sure you have one handy for when you come out of the bath. Pat your vulva dry with tissues or loo paper before you put it on. If your thighs become sore from wearing sanitary towels, dab them with talcum powder.

Remember to change your towel or tampon regularly – three or four times a day, and maybe even more during the first few days. Menstrual blood begins to smell slightly when it reaches the air and the warmth of your body increases the smell.

If your pants get blood on them, the best way to get rid of the stains is to soak and rub them in cold, salty water before you wash them.

Look after your skin
The hormones whizzing around your body make your skin glands particularly active. The extra oil they produce can clog the pores and give you spots on your face and sometimes your back as well.

The simplest way to unclog pores is to wash your face morning and night with medicated soap and warm water. Then use a toning lotion to tighten up

I HAVE REALLY BAD
SKIN AROUND THE
TIME OF MY PERIODS

the pores again. If your face is sensitive to soap, buy a medicated face lotion or cream from a chemist.

Some experts have suggested that people with spots should avoid fatty and greasy foods, such as chocolate, chips, and cheese and eat plenty of fresh fruit instead. Others think that foods have nothing to do with spots. Experiment for yourself to see if there's a particular food that makes you come out in spots. If so, avoid it!

It's very tempting to pick and squeeze spots. Don't – it may only make them worse! If all else fails, put a dab of medicated make-up on the worst ones and try to forget about them.

Care for your hair

My hair's gone
all greasy.

At puberty, the oil glands in your scalp that keep your hair healthy often start working overtime, and make your hair greasy instead. Choose a shampoo for

CHOOSE A SHAMPOO FOR GREASY HAIR,
GIVE YOUR HAIR ONLY ONE LATHERING
AND MAKE SURE YOU RINSE ALL THE
SHAMPOO OUT.

greasy hair, give your hair only one lathering and make sure you rinse all the shampoo out. Your hair should squeak when it's clean!

Sleep well

> I seem to need
> more sleep
> than I used to.

You may find that your sleep pattern is changing. Your own rhythm is what suits you best – don't fight it or compare it with your friends. People need different amounts of sleep. You might need nine or ten hours a night, while a friend might need only seven or eight hours, or the other way round. If you find you're particularly tired during your periods, have some early nights.

If you have problems getting to sleep, it may be that your body doesn't need as much sleep as you think. It's better to stay up or read in bed until you feel sleepy, rather than going to bed and worrying about not being able to get to sleep. You may find that a cup of camomile tea or warm milk helps calm you down. If you can't get to sleep because you're worrying about a problem, try to share it with someone. Fresh air and exercise during the day will always help you sleep better.

Too much sleep, on the other hand, can make you feel just as bad as not enough. Don't stay in bed longer than you need, particularly if you have period cramps. It'll only make you feel worse.

Rest is just as important as sleep. Try to find half an hour or more every day to relax, however pressured you may feel. Lie flat on the floor and let your muscles relax one by one or sit in a chair and concentrate on a spot on the wall. Alternatively, go for a walk and concentrate on breathing, not on thinking, or lie on your bed with your eyes closed and listen to some relaxing music.

Shape up

There have been a number of recent 'shock horror' stories in the newspapers about how unfit teenagers are becoming. Don't let yourself be one of them! Daily exercises, even if only for five minutes, will help your body stay in good shape. If you can do twenty minutes of aerobic exercises three times a week, even better. As well as keeping you in tip-top shape, they may also help period pains.

I'D LIKE TO BE REALLY FIT

Tennis, swimming and aerobics are all good exercise. But if organized sports aren't locally available or aren't your idea of fun, there are plenty of other ways to keep fit. Run up and down the stairs five times a day; take the dog for a long walk every morning; dance to your favourite music; go for a cycle ride with a friend.

You can tone some of your muscles even while you're sitting down. Clench your buttock and thigh muscles; press your feet into the floor; circle your arms round and around; swing your head gently in a circle, first one way and then the other.

Whatever exercises you choose to do, try to do them regularly. Don't find an excuse to give up. If you start to find them boring, try doing them with a friend or in time to music. If you exercise at the same time every day, say when you get up, it will become as much of a habit as brushing your teeth or washing your face.

An exercise routine

If you do get period pains, then it's a good idea to do extra exercises to loosen and relax you. The following exercises are designed to strengthen your tummy and pelvic muscles and should relieve cramps. You might not notice any difference for the first month or so, but if you do the exercises regularly, they should start being effective.

Exercise 1

Repeat ten times.

Stand straight with your feet apart and your arms stretched out at shoulder height.

Keeping your arms straight, swing your right hand down to touch your left foot. Come back to your starting position.

Then swing your left hand down to touch your right foot.

Exercise 2

Repeat ten times.

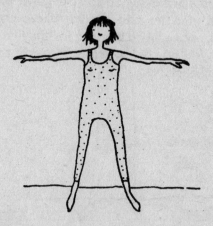

Stand in the same starting position as for Exercise 1.

Twist your body and right arm to the left, without moving your feet. Keep both arms straight and at shoulder height. Return to the starting position and then twist your body and left arm to the right.

Exercise 3

Repeat ten times.

Stand with your feet apart and your arms stretched straight above your head.

Keeping your knees straight, bend down and touch your toes. Return to the starting position with your arms still at full stretch.

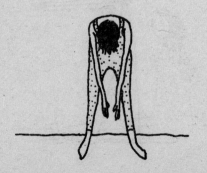

Exercise 4

Repeat ten times.

Sit on the floor with your legs and feet together and your knees straight. Put your hands on your shoulders.

Stretch forward and put your fingers on your toes (if you can't reach them at first, bend your knees).

Return to the starting position.

Exercise 5

Repeat five times.

Kneel up with your hands flat on the floor. Breathe in slowly. As you breathe out, hump your back, pull in your tummy muscles and look down towards your knees.

Now breathe in. As you do so, lift your head upwards and arch your back at the same time. Keep your arms straight the whole time.

Exercise 6

Sit on your heels with your arms in front of you. Gradually stretch forward until your tummy is stretched right over your legs, your forehead is touching the floor and your arms are stretched as far as they will go. Relax, and breathe deeply.

Enjoy eating

In the year before your periods start, it's quite likely that you'll put on about five kilos. In the following two years, you may put on another 3.5–5.5 kilos a year until you reach your adult weight. This weight gain is absolutely normal. It does *not* mean you're going to end up fat. You'll be growing taller and your limbs will be growing longer at the same time.

You need to eat enough to grow properly and to give you energy for everything you do. Some girls worry so much about their weight, that they starve themselves (anorexics) or stuff themselves and then throw up (bulimics). Strict diets and crash diets aren't a good idea when you're growing, as they can permanently harm your body and upset your menstrual cycle.

If you want to keep yourself in trim, just remember these three things: Eat plenty of fresh fruit and vegetables; limit sugary and high fat foods like chocolate, cake and biscuits; and exercise regularly.

Chapter 7
What If . . . ?
(Queries about periods)

Periods should be no more bother than eating, sleeping or going to the toilet, but sometimes people have worries about them. If you think you have a problem, share it with someone — don't keep it to yourself. The sooner someone can help you, the less time you'll spend worrying.

What if I have a vaginal discharge?

You're quite likely to have a vaginal discharge before a period and also when you ovulate (mid-way between periods). A normal vaginal discharge is a small amount of white or colourless fluid.

But, if your discharge changes in any of the following ways, it's worth telling someone close to you or going to see a doctor:

➤ If it becomes discoloured (yellow and blood-stained) and smelly. First check you haven't left a tampon in.
➤ If it becomes much thicker and heavier.
➤ If you get a constant sore, burning or itching feeling.

A doctor can quickly tell whether a discharge is normal or not. You may have nothing wrong at all. Or, you may have a common infection called Thrush, which can be easily treated.

What if my periods haven't started yet?

(Doctors call this *amenorrhea* – pronounced a-men-or-eea.)

If you haven't started your periods yet and most of your friends have, don't worry. It doesn't mean you won't. It just means your body timetable is different from theirs. Sometimes girls don't start until they're sixteen or seventeen. But in the end, everyone does, just like these two girls eventually did.

I started developing early, with the exception of my periods. My mum told me all about them when I was ten and gave me some sanitary towels to put away until I needed them — but nothing happened. I had my first bra, but still no periods. I wondered if I was normal. The longer I waited, the more I worried about what could be wrong. At first, only a few of my friends started, then almost all of them. Everyone assumed I'd started, so I couldn't confide in anyone.

My mum told me not to worry, so did the doctor. But short of proof that everything was OK, nothing could calm my fears. Every time I had something like a tummy ache, I thought my periods were starting, but they never did. I had all sorts of fantasies about what was wrong. The doctor couldn't find anything wrong at all. When I was fifteen, she told me to wait another six months and eat plenty of oranges (for vitamin C). Finally, three months later, I had my first period — what an anti-climax. I was nearly sixteen.

My periods didn't begin until I was over seventeen. As far as my friends were concerned, I'd started three years before, when most of them began theirs. For three years I'd lived this lie, because I didn't want them to laugh at me for being a late starter. I couldn't think why I didn't have periods like them. I kept quiet about it for ages.

Then I noticed that every so often my friends would ask to be excused from swimming and showers after games. Ah ha! So every so often I'd do the same. The times I chose to be excused, I'd also make a point of complaining of tummy ache and all the other things my friends seemed to do.

Unfortunately for me, we had a PE teacher who kept a note of who was excused showers and when. She mentioned to the school doctor, on a check-up visit, that my periods were totally irregular. I was found out. I had to admit that it was all a pretence. I felt better, though, having told someone. It wasn't long after this that my periods actually started.

Once I'd started and saw what was involved, I wondered why I'd ever been so anxious to start!

What if my periods are heavy?

Although the flow may look only like blood, in fact blood makes up only half of it. The rest includes the remains of the extra lining of the uterus and sticky mucus from the cervix and vagina.

The amount of blood you lose is actually very little – the equivalent of between four and eight table-spoons – even if it looks a lot more.

How much blood there is varies from person to person and month to month. If there's a good deal of blood, that's just as healthy as not very much (your body soon replaces whatever blood you lose).

Periods are considered heavy if:

➤ You need (rather than choose) to use more than six towels or tampons a day, every day of your period.
➤ Your period lasts for much more than a week.
➤ You have more than one period a month and you feel tired and sleepy, even though you're eating well and sleeping normally.

Heavy periods can be caused by shock or worry or upset to your normal routine – such as changing schools, going on holiday and so on. On the other hand, they could mean that your uterus is not work-ing quite the way it should. If your period suddenly becomes heavier and you can't think of a good reason, it is a good idea to see a doctor.

The doctor might suggest that you eat extra amounts of some iron-rich foods, such as brown bread, liver and watercress, or might prescribe iron tablets.

What if my periods come late or skip a month?
More often than not, for the first two years or so, your periods may be irregular. This is because you haven't started ovulating (see page 33). Hormones send messages to make the lining of your uterus thicken, but the messages are often erratic.

As your ovaries mature, you'll begin ovulating – not necessarily every month at first, maybe every two or three. Once you ovulate regularly every month or so, you should notice a more definite pattern to your cycle, and your periods will probably become heavier.

Lots of things can upset your cycle, such as illness or an emotional upset, sudden changes, such as travelling, moving school or house, hard physical work, exams or a crash diet.

Your periods might stop completely for a while, or you may have lighter or heavier periods than usual. After a break, you might find that your cycle becomes longer or shorter than it was before.

Once you have a regular cycle, you need worry about irregular periods only if:

➤ The pattern changes for no good reason and becomes much heavier or lighter.
➤ You miss two periods in a row – and there's no chance of your being pregnant – or if you miss one period and think you might be pregnant.

It's worth going to the doctor for a check-up about either of these.

What if I have bleeding between periods (spotting)?

If you notice any bleeding between periods, you should always see a doctor about it, because it's not a usual thing to happen. If it's only light spotting during the middle of the cycle, it's probably to do with ovulation. At this time, some people have a slight pain in either the right or left side of their tummy. This is a sign that the egg is leaving the ovary. However, if the pain lasts for more than a day or so, it might be a sign of illness, so it's worth going to see a doctor about it.

What if I feel faint during my period?

Occasionally, girls feel faint during their periods. If this happens to you, have some early nights and avoid standing up for long stretches of time – sit down or walk around instead.

When you feel faint, sit down with your head beveen your knees until you feel better, and then have a drink of cold water. Alternatively, lie flat on the floor with either your feet resting on a chair, or your bent knees hugged towards your chest.

What if my breasts feel sore during a period?

Sore breasts are quite common before and during a period. It doesn't mean anything is wrong with them. Fluid builds up in them as a result of hormone changes and may make them feel more tender. After the period, the breasts go back to normal.

Before a period, my breasts get bigger
and my nipples get sore. I have to
wear a bigger bra.

Usually for a week before my period
my breasts feel very lumpy and
tender.

These changes often go completely unnoticed. If they
bother you, wear a slightly bigger bra and have a soak
in a warm bath.

On the whole your breasts won't feel lumpy after a
period. If they do, it may be normal, but you would be
wise to see a doctor.

What if I get cramps and other pains?

Before you start ovulating, it's unlikely, though not
impossible, that you'll have painful periods. Once
ovulation happens regularly you might start having
cramps and pains during periods, but not necessarily.
In any case, people feel pain quite differently – what
one person can bear may be unbearable to someone
else.

Many people have discomfort rather than pains:

I get a dragging feeling, but it isn't
real pain. I also feel constipated and
have a feeling of fullness in the first
few days of a period.

I can feel my uterus contracting and tension building up. My stomach feels heavy and aches.

Some people, however, have quite severe pains:

Usually on the first day, I have a lot of pain and an upset tummy. I feel sick (often bad enough to have to go to bed for most of the day).

The pain is usually to do with the period, but not always. You might be constipated as well. If so, try to eat foods with plenty of fibre (such as brown bread, fruit, salads and raw vegetables). Or it may be because you're worried about your periods. Worry can make you tense and knotted up and makes the pain seem worse. It may even be that you get pain, because you're expecting it:

I often get bad cramps, but if I pretend I haven't got them they go away.

If you do get pains, don't just grit your teeth and bear them. There are plenty of things you can do to relieve them. Overleaf are some people's suggestions. Try some of them out and see which work best for you.

If the pain is more than you can bear, go to your doctor and ask for advice. There are several medical ways of helping period cramps.

I GO FOR A WALK, DRINK LOTS OF WATER AND HAVE SOME EARLY NIGHTS.

I MAKE SURE I EAT WELL TO KEEP UP MY ENERGY. I ALSO TAKE VITAMIN C.

I HUG A HOT-WATER BOTTLE AGAINST MY TUMMY. I TRY NOT TO MOVE AROUND TOO MUCH. SIT UP STRAIGHT INSTEAD OF SITTING IN MY USUAL SLOPPY WAY AND MAYBE TAKE A PAIN-KILLER.

IF I CAN I EXERCISE, WHICH ISN'T AT ALL GOOD AT FIRST, BUT IF I SURVIVE, THEN IT'S VERY GOOD!

I MASSAGE MY STOMACH AND BACK. I FIND IT HELPFUL TO PRESS AND RUB THE BOTTOM OF MY SPINE WITH MY KNUCKLES OR FINGERTIPS.

I TRY TO RELAX AND BREATHE DEEPLY.

USUALLY I LIE ON MY BACK WITH MY KNEES UP.

I TAKE A LONG BATH AND GO TO BED WITH A CUP OF TEA. SOMETIMES LYING ON MY TUMMY HELPS.

Chapter 8
Free Booklets and Samples

The following firms produce leaflets, offer samples of their products and have an advisory service you might like to write to if you have a particular problem or question.

The Marion Cooper Advisory Service Centre,
Alum Rock Road,
Birmingham,
B8 3DZ.

(Booklet: *What's Happening – The Inside Story*)

Tambrands Ltd,
Dunsbury Way,
Havant,
Hampshire,
PO9 5DG.

(Booklets: *Talking about You* and *A Time for Answers*)

Simplicity Advisory Service,
Kimberley-Clark Ltd,
Larkfield,
Aylesford,
Kent,
ME20 7PS.

(Pack containing booklets: *Very Personally Yours* and *Growing Up Young*.
Life Cycle series – a set of eight leaflets)

Sancella Advisory Service,
Scott House,
Wood St,
East Grinstead,
RH19 1UR.

(Booklet: *Girltalk*)

Further Reading on Health and Sex Education

Girls' and Boys' Questions Answered. National Marriage Guidance Council, 1980.

Parents and Teachers. Open University. Harper and Row, 1982.

What's Happening To Me? Peter Mayle. Macmillan, 1991.

Understanding the Facts of Life. Susan Meredith and Robyn Gee. Usborne, 1985

Further Reading

Growing Up: Facts of Life. Susan Meredith.
Usborne, 1985.

Girltalk. (Pan) Carol Weston, Macmillan,
revised 1993.

Growing Up Series (set of three booklets),
Family Planning Association, 1991

What's Happening to my Body? A growing-up guide for
parents and daughters, Lynda Madaras,
Penguin, 1989

What's Happening to my Body? A growing-up guide for
parents and sons, Lynda Madaras,
Penguin, 1989

Other books you will enjoy from
Macmillan

Anita Naik
My Body, Myself

The Ultimate Health Book for Girls

Anita Naik, *Just Seventeen*'s resident agony aunt, sweeps away the myths and fiction surrounding the constant changes affecting the female body.

My Body, Myself gives clear and informative advice on everything you will ever want or need to know about your body and emotions.

Carol Weston
Girltalk

All the things your sister never told you!

If you want to flirt but not seem a fool, break up with your man without breaking down, or say no to a creep without being rude, read the chapter on 'Love'. Turn to 'Sex' to learn what you should know before saying yes or no. Flip to 'Family' to discover how to cope with parents who were never young themselves. And if you want to make money, build a career, get on at school or get some unbiased advice about drink or drugs, it's all here.

Girltalk – everything you wanted to know about life but sometimes find it hard to ask about. Don't leave home without it!

Michele Elliott
The Willow Street Kids

It's your right to be safe!

What would you do if:

Someone tried to bully you?

A stranger approached you in the street?

You saw thick black smoke coming from a neighbour's house?

A friend offered you money to steal from a shop?

An older person you know tried to touch you in a way which made you feel uncomfortable?

The Willow Street Kids know what to do! They stick together and help each other deal with some very tricky problems. Their adventures and dilemmas will help you figure out what to do if any of the things that happen to them ever happens to you or to a friend.

The Willow Street Kids is unique because the stories in the book are all true and have been told by children to whom they have happened.

Celia Rees
The Bailey Game

'Every school has places that you can find if you want to, if you don't want people to see you, if you need somewhere private. That had been important in the Bailey Game – privacy and being secret.'

The Bailey Game was vicious, it wrecked people's lives; but two years ago, it was all anyone in Alex Lewis' class thought or talked about. Until one terrifying day in early spring. What happened then should have been enough to stop anyone ever wanting to play the Game again – ever.

Now a new girl, Lauren Price, has arrived at the school. She is new, she is different, and she comes from somewhere else. That is enough. The Bailey Game is about to start.

Alex finds she has some tough choices to make in a world where being on the outside can be dangerous . . .

"An exciting and disturbing tale . . . I highly recommend *The Bailey Game*."

Michele Elliott, *KIDSCAPE*

A selected list of titles available from Macmillan and Pan Books

The prices shown below are correct at the time of going to press. However, Macmillan Publishers reserve the right to show new retail prices on covers which may differ from those previously advertised.

Anita Naik		
My Body, Myself	0 330 34333 5	£4.99
Carol Weston		
Girltalk	0 330 32803 4	£5.99
Michele Elliott		
<u>The Willow Street Kids</u>		
Be Smart, Stay Safe	0 330 35184 2	£3.99
Beat the Bullies	0 330 35185 0	£3.99
Celia Rees		
The Bailey Game	0 330 33326 7	£3.50

All Macmillan titles can be ordered at your local bookshop or are available by post from:

Book Service by Post
PO Box 29, Douglas, Isle of Man IM99 1BQ

Credit cards accepted. For details:
Telephone: 01624 675137
Fax: 01624 670923
E-mail: bookshop@enterprise.net

Free postage and packing in the UK.
Overseas customers: add £1 per book (paperback)
and £3 per book (hardback).